HUGGING A CLOUD

PROFITS + MEANING
FROM THE HUMAN SIDE OF BUSINESS

PETE GEISSLER

IN COLLABORATION WITH
JIM BROWNE, DON NUSSER, BILL
O'ROURKE, DENNIS SLEVIN, AND BARRY WOLFE.

The Expressive Press
www.TheExpressivePress.com

ISBN-13: 978-1517189358
ISBN-10: 1517189357

Other books by Pete Geissler and The Expressive Press

- The Power of Writing Well
- The Power of Being Articulate
- The Power of Ethics, with Bill O'Rourke
- The Power of Dignity
- Divorce can be Such Sweet Sorrow
- Bigshots' Bull*!@#
- An Accidental Life

Other books from The Expressive Press

- VB.Net Web Development, by Dr. Charles Wood
- The Little Black Book of Human Resources Management, by Barry Wolfe

Table of Contents

5

PROLOGUE:
WHY THIS BOOK IS IMPORTANT

Perhaps the biggest lie in business is "If you can't measure it, you can't manage it." Of course that simple aphorism has been proven wrong many times. John Wanamaker, the retail magnate, is famous for saying: "I spend a lot of money on advertising and I know half of it is wasted. Trouble is, I don't know which half." The same is true of accounting, law, and even top management.

Hugging a Cloud acknowledges that fact of business life, and goes a step further:

The human side of business is difficult or impossible to measure, but it cannot be ignored.

Leaders cannot afford to ignore the thinking, behaviors, and relationships that define the human side of business. All, separately and together, contribute in some way to profits+meaning. And they can be measured--perhaps not as precisely as financial ratios can be measured--with simple metrics that create the Profits+Meaning Index, or PMI.

PMI, when combined with financial ratios, realistically evaluates the short- and long-term efficiency and prospects of a business and its leadership. Enlightened and forward-thinking leaders will hug the cloud that is the human side of business.

PART I:
ELEVATING EVALUATIONS TO BEYOND FINANCE

"The secret of change is to focus all of your energy not on fighting the old, but on building the new."
Socrates

Leaders are constantly torn between the obvious need to stick with traditional ways of thinking and evaluating performance with the equally obvious need to change them. Perhaps this balancing act is most apparent when evaluating the needs for short -term performance, aka quarterly and yearly financial ratios, with long-term performance, aka strategies that may or may not pay off with improved financial ratios for several years or decades. Embracing the cloud that is the human side of business and applying the Profits+Meaning Index, combined with traditional financial ratios, gives equal weight to both needs.

1. A Modest proposal for a new, more sustainable way to evaluate leadership

The Profits+Meaning Index; balancing short- and long term interests

"We badly need a new measure for economic success that goes beyond earnings per share." Paul Roberts,1939-, American economist and co-founder of Reaganomics, in his book *The Impulse Society: America in the Age of Instant Gratification.*

The human side--the side that is difficult to measure but impossible to ignore-- is the future of business; it complements but does not replace the hard side--the side that can be measured and is equally impossible to ignore.

The **Profits +Meaning Index (PMI),** a way to quantify the effectiveness of leaders to embrace and implement the thinking and behaviors described in this book. It enables stakeholders, analysts, and others to simultaneously evaluate the long- and short-term prospects of a business.

NOTE: Meaning *in the context of this book is that euphoric state of mind that is derived from knowing that what you are doing is useful, beneficial to all stakeholders in a business and to society, and sustainable. It eschews short-term thinking and behaviors.*

The PMI tracks and defines the stability and growth of three groups of people, each of whom is far more expensive to attract, hold, and utilize than is capital. Each is, therefore, a more credible, influential, and accurate indicator and evaluator of management acumen and efficiency. The three groups can be discussed separately, but, in the real world, they are inextricably dependent upon each other:

- **Employees** are the sources of all intelligence and innovation needed to differentiate a business and create markets, customers, revenue, and profit. Productive employees can be enticed to stay in their jobs with proper compensation--e.g. bonuses for retaining and growing the customer base-- and proper treatment from the top, e.g. with manifest dignity, safety, ethics, integrity, trust, and other desirable human characteristics.

  Employees are not usually terminated or mired in dead-end jobs, and firms do not stagnate or perform below expectations, because they lack the technical skills that are taught so well in colleges. Nevertheless, t he dominance of technical skills in curricula seems to be increasing: Witness the STEM revolution that has enamored politicians from the President to all his minions and to academicians at all levels and that is based on near-term job openings.

Such thinking promotes short -term management at the expense of long-term sustainability. Consider that employees are terminated or passed over for promotion, and firms stagnate and/or disappear, because they lack such human-side skills as the ability to communicate, to treat others with the respect they deserve, to behave ethically, to be polite, and so on ... the skills that are explored in this book and which are ignored or de-emphasized by our colleges.

- **Customers** are the sources of virtually all funds needed to hire employees and to purchase the materials and services needed to support them. They can be enticed to stay with continuous improvements in a firm's products and services, the function of management policies and employees who implement them. It almost goes without saying that customers stay with a supplier when they are satisfied with its products and services; it is perhaps less obvious that customers stay with a supplier because they are happy with the personalities and behaviors--ethics, dignity and the like-- of the people with whom they interact-- and their confidence in management to sustain the business via continuous improvements with long-term strategies.

- **Stockholders** are the sources of capital who can be enticed to hold their investments, thereby avoiding expensive churning (a goal might be to increase the average holding of about ten months now to, say, five years) with proper communications of management's strategies for long-term growth via innovations, again the function of employees. Long-term holdings can be encouraged further by a Tobin Tax, a hefty tax on short-term transactions designed to stabilize financial markets and could also stabilize holdings in an individual firm. Another way could be to reward shareholders, employees, and customers for loyalty by gifting or lowering the price of shares in targeted, long-term development of, say, new products that could open new markets.

Calculating the PMI and interpreting its implications: Data for the constancy and/or change in the three people groups are readily available at most firms, enabling PMI to be calculated easily. For example, a PMI of 1.0 would indicate a firm that has stagnated and investors might hold or sell shares, employees would look for greener pastures, and customers might look for new suppliers. A PMI higher than 1.0 indicates a firm that is growing profitably, its strategies are working, and investors would buy or hold shares; and of lower than 1.0 a firm that is shrinking, its strategies are failing, investors might sell shares, and employees and customers would lose confidence in management and find other opportunities.

NOTE: The authors are fully aware that the above procedure for calculating the PMI is abstract, incomplete, and simplistic. Nevertheless, a more detailed explanation/procedure is beyond the scope and purpose of this book, which is to encourage the thinking and behaviors that result in a positive PMI. The development, use, and refinement of metrics is a separate topic that is best left to the appropriate experts in the various disciplines. Readers can, nevertheless, examine traditional sustainability metrics via the Global Reporting Initiative, the Dow Jones Sustainability Index, and similar sites.

Profiling Human-Side Leaders

Please note that technical skills are conspicuously missing from the following profiles, which does not mean that leaders lack 'hard' skills. They in fact tend to excel in those skills as well.

The human side and leadership are linked so tightly as to be one: For example, executives cannot lead if they cannot clearly articulate their vision and values in both words and actions, or if they are perceived to be callous, unethical, self-centered and with similar character flaws.

Human-Side Leaders tend to possess the many attributes for personal and professional success. They are educated, intelligent, insightful, experienced, and flexible. In addition, they communicate clearly, honestly, and as needed (they do not over- or under-communicate); they exude confidence and optimism so that others feel good about themselves and the firm; they are humble and empathetic, able to understand and appreciate other's viewpoints and opinions; they are available to others, especially during trying times; they are constructive, fair, and objective when evaluating the performance of others; they are committed to the long-term success of the firm and its employees, and demonstrate that commitment in words and actions; they are ethical at all times and in every situation; they know that safety first is a meaningful way of life, not a meaningless slogan; and they treat others with respect and dignity, and insist that they be treated similarly. They are positive almost to a fault. They encourage and coach others, and are a constant source of energy and enthusiasm for all stakeholders.

Human-side leaders also:

- Strive to improve the lives of others by being generous, unselfish, humanitarian, and benevolent;
- Deal with people objectively and fairly by being understanding, impartial, equitable, and unbiased;
- Relate to people in commendable ways by being friendly, gracious, cordial, and kind; and
- Act out of concern for others by being sympathetic, considerate, even-handed, and honorable.

Others have described successful leaders as magnanimous, humble, prudent, courageous, principled, fair, and visionary. They exhibit these traits by aligning their actions with words that are expressed clearly, purposefully, and truthfully.

A bit of history that adds validity to The PMI

Business has lived through many subsets of the false god of managing for financial ratios. *Productivity* started the ball rolling in the 1970s. It was followed quickly by *Quality*, and then *Productivity and Quality* were rolled into one subset called *Total Quality Management*, which was refined into *Six Sigma*, which was ennobled by Jack Welch and General Electric and so became the apex of subsets. Then along came *Supply Chain Management, Speed, Lean and Mean,* and *Information* as competitive advantages, aka enhancers of revenue and profit. They were followed by a plethora of also-rans espoused by various consultants: *Re-engineering, Paradigm Shift, Restructuring,* and *Continuous Learning.* Then, most recently and most damaging and misguided, *Stockholder Value* and *Profitable Growth.*

Each subset has its assets and liabilities, its advocates and enemies. For example, higher productivity is an asset until employees are stretched beyond tolerable limits. And stockholder value is wonderful as long as it doesn't lead to greed, usually at the top, which has led to perverse, short-term decisions that have destroyed companies and lives. All the subsets of the past have one glaring flaw: They ignore people, and people are "our most important assets." Ask any leader.

Embracing a cloud remedies that flaw.

Adding still more validity to the PMI

The National Association of Colleges and Employers asked employers to name the top ten attributes they want in employees, eight of the ten are on the soft side: Able to verbally communicate; work in a team; make decisions and solve problems; plan, organize, and prioritize work; obtain and process information; analyze quantitative data; create and edit written documents; and to influence others.

Tucked in the seventh and eighth slots are technical knowledge and proficiency with computer programs.

In short, colleges turn out brilliantly trained technicians who are ill-equipped for optimizing their potential for productive and meaningful lives.

2. Capital is no longer king

Financial ratios have lost their strangle hold on evaluations

Evaluating a business and its management using financial ratios--by how efficiently capital is utilized-- such as ROE, ROS, PE, RONA hasn't led to realistic conclusions regarding performance or strategy, aka sustainability, of managers, leaders, or firms. The truth behind that statement lies in the many well-documented failures of the nineties and early 2000s, as well as in the more obscure, but no less spectacular failures of Westinghouse and Dravo Corporation, both icons of stability before their boards succumbed to managing for profitable growth or stockholder value. More recently are the lackluster performances of such firms as Hewlett Packard, Bank of America, and General Motors.

The bottom line is that evaluating by financial ratios is based on an ongoing fallacy: that capital is scarce and costly.

It isn't now, it hasn't been for at least five years, and likely won't be for many years into the future, a happy result of the laws of supply and demand. At this time--mid- 2015--business is awash in inexpensive capital, as it has been since 2010. Its cost is so low that it can be either ignored or given passing importance in any evaluation of performance. For credence: A recent study by Bain & Company concludes that we have entered an era of capital superabundance: total financial assets are ten times the value of global output of all goods and services, and it will grow by fifty percent to 15 times global output by 2020. In contrast, it was only 7 in 2000.

In a related phenomenon, many managers/leaders yearn to focus on long-term performance but don't think it is an option, fearing pressure from investors clamoring for short-term results and prompting the question: who's running the business? Its leaders? Security analysts? Vocal stockholders?

These two forces--the lingering plentitude and low cost of capital and a longing for long-term management--have converged to force a new way to evaluate performance. Thoughtful academicians and managers can spearhead the change by integrating the **Profits +Meaning Index--PMI**--into evaluations, giving PMI equal weight with financial ratios, thus enabling managers, other employees, shareholders, and other stakeholders to consider the long- and short-term impacts of decisions.

PART II:
CLEAR THINKING VIA INTUITION AND DISCIPLINE

"**Progression, growth, and happiness are the natural consequences of good ideas. Stagnation, depression, and unhappiness are the consequences of bad ideas.**" Richard Weaver, in his groundbreaking book, *Ideas Have Consequences.*

Intelligence is use of the intellect to understand, know, to be able to solve and resolve, to be able to discover new insights that others can't. Beyond basics, intelligence is the ability to understand more quickly and deeply than others. Speed and timing enter the definition.

3. Sustainability: What is it? Is it possible?

The many confusing definitions and uses...the focus on environmental responsibility and the built environment...the benefits of practicing sustainability

Sustainability can be broadly defined as operating and behaving in ways that preserve and/or extend the long-term quality and productive capacity of the natural and social environments. *Competitive advantage* can be broadly defined as any activity that creates value that is superior to those offered by competitors.

Sustainable competitive advantage is created when customers perceive a firm's products and/or services as more valuable than alternatives; the products/services cannot easily be duplicated, replaced, or imitated by others; and they are not commonplace.

The appropriate and thoughtful implementation of sustainability into everyday business practices:

- Enhances a firm's image, attracting like-minded employees, customers, and shareholders;

- Increases profitability via lower consumption of energy and raw materials and their associated costs; and, least important in the current business climate...
- Opens/expands access to capital: Loans are long-term agreements; it follows that that banks are more willing to loan to firms that they feel are more efficient and understand that sustainability will pay off in the long run.

Despite its abilities to lower some costs, sustainable competitive advantage cannot be linked directly and quantifiably to higher profitability, which doesn't stop forward-thinking leaders from embracing the principles. For example, only 24% of all respondents (72% of executives) to an *Economist* survey agree that sustainability raises profitability in the short term, but 69% (93% of executives) say it will in the long term. One can easily conclude from those data alone that sustainability will be a guiding principle of leadership in the foreseeable future, perhaps because it will prepare firms for more strict environmental laws and the social risks of dealing with carbon emissions and climate change.

Responsible leaders will avoid overselling sustainability by claiming that it will not impair the future use of resources or will not limit the availability of resources to future generations (everything we do and build impairs and limits in some way); will eliminate use of carbon-based fuels (not attainable in the near future); will slow global warming and the resultant climate change (the debate will go on for years); and any claim containing the word "green", another ambiguous word.

Responsible leaders will focus on the relative aspects of sustainability and its potential to reduce costs and the impact of actions on the environment, and enhance the quality of life. Competitive advantage will be strengthened by applying the best and most appropriate elements of sustainability in day-to-day business operations, and in products and services.

4. Intelligence is your only product: it creates progress and competitive advantage

The results of intelligence--or its lack-- are expressed in words, pictures (drawings, e.g.), and products...the roles of insight, creativity, and honesty

*"Ideas shape the course of history."*John Maynard Keynes. *"Ideas shape the course of careers and firms".* The authors. *"The difference between intelligence and education is this: intelligence will make you a good living."* Charles Kettering, 1876-1958, American inventor and businessman.

Businesses of all types—whether categorized as manufacturing or service—market nothing more than their individual or collective Intelligence. It—or its lack-- is displayed by products, services, words, and pictures, and it separates winners from losers.

We intuitively know intelligence when we experience it: the person who grasps and analyzes the situation at hand quickly and clearly communicates his or her understandings and conclusions; he or she demonstrates superior perceptions and verbal skills. Whether correctly or erroneously, we label those who don't, can't, or won't as not too bright, slow, and lacking credibility—exactly the labels that will destroy employees and firms in a heartbeat.

Intelligence has three components, all rare in business and society:

1. Insight into the needs and wants of customers, created by active listening to understand. GIGO (Garbage In, Garbage Out) applies to the human mind as much as computers.
2. Creativity to convert insight into solutions that meet needs and wants most expeditiously and economically. Creativity was defined by Edwin Land, the inventor of instant photography, as the cessation of stupidity, or, on the other side of that coin, the perpetuation of intelligence.
3. Honesty to openly communicate accurately, clearly, concisely, and truthfully. *Knowledge is power* is a useless and misleading aphorism if knowledge isn't communicated.

Businesses convey their intelligence or its lack via products, ads, papers, speeches, proposals, reports, letters, brochures, web sites ,meetings and so on. Their overarching purpose is to paint themselves as more intelligent than competitors; nothing will enhance that purpose more quickly and thoroughly than clear, concise, on-point English and design. Your communications—all of them and which include your products-- are the clearest and most enduring reflections of your intelligence.

5. Results writing and communications: The essential expression of Intelligence

Good writing defined by traits and results...every business needs a voice...the psychic and financial rewards...the deeper reasons to write well

"Highly accomplished people use language in an instinctive or intuitive way--and it's focused on what they're trying to accomplish. "Jerry Porras, Stewart Emery, and Mark Thompson in *Success Built to Last.*

"...writing is primarily an exercise in logic and words are just the tools designed to do a specific job." William Zinsser, *in Writing to Learn.*

To reiterate: All businesses, regardless of their expertise or discipline, thrive or fail solely on their intellects—the capacity for knowledge and rational thought. Every intellect requires a voice; without it, nobody knows that the intellect exists, or whether it is superior or inferior to others'.

For example, every engineering consultant's/department's voice is primarily its drawings (the hard side of engineering), related and supporting documents, whether electronic or paper, and presentations (the human side). When the voices on both sides express clear, concise, creative, on-point, logical thinking, the voices create competitive advantage for individuals and firms; when it doesn't, it creates competitive weakness.

The business persons I've met invariably tell me that they hate to communicate, especially to write. They say that they communicate badly, spend—some say "waste"-- thirty to ninety percent of their time doing it, and would rather be working on the hard side, where they're more comfortable. Managers wish wistfully that employees could write and speak better, but they struggle to articulate what better is, why it is important, or even to recognize it.

Better communications, both internal and external, are recognized and known by their traits and results. Their traits are clarity (the message is understood after one careful reading or listening); concision (the message contains only those thoughts and words needed to meet the purpose(s) of readers or listeners, aka receivers); and logic (thoughts are arranged in a sequence that is clear to receivers without excursions to other thoughts).

The result of better communications is higher **profitability**, a claim that is supported by surveys of managers that indicated that profits would jump by one to ten percent of sales if all communications did their jobs efficiently. Higher profitability is the direct result of noticeably and measurably higher ...

- **productivity** of all employees, including and especially managers, by eliminating or minimizing the tag games that are inevitably caused by murky communications that require editing/rewriting or clarifying by higher authorities;
- **hit rates and lower sales/marketing costs** that result from proposals and reports that are quickly, easily, and accurately interpreted and evaluated by customers; and
- **rates of repeat business** from customers that understand and respect your intellect; you cannot keep customers that don't, and losing and replacing one costs at least ten to fifty times more than keeping one.

The disciplines of writing comprise the foundation of all your communications.

The methodical, evolving process of writing actually forces new thoughts to emerge from your mind, allowing you to make sense of your surroundings, your life, and, on a smaller scale, the document that you are composing at the moment.

In essence, better writing gives your mind a disciplined means of expression and conjuring up that great idea that separates the ordinary from the extraordinary, another basis for your competitive advantage. It is a way to discover what you are thinking. Jeff Bezos, the legendary guru behind Amazon, agrees: "There is no way to write a ... memo without clear thinking." Perhaps E. M. Forster, an English novelist and short story writer, said it best:" How do I know what I think until I see what I say?"

Practice These Three Quick Tips For Communicating Better

To reflect your true intellect, become a careful, critical reader. Nothing destroys your credibility more than nonsensical sentences. Avoid this, from a technical paper: *Typical annual volumes reached 8,250,000 gallons per month at a cost of $27,000.* What are the annual volumes and cost? And this from a newsletter on healthy living: *Exercising and eating well can lower your risk of dying.* How's that for wishful thinking?

To be on point, understand your receivers' needs and wants as specifically as possible and avoid veering away from them. In general, your receivers are always busy, harassed, and unwilling to waste time with irrelevant and murky prose that needs to be encoded, so get to your point quickly, clearly, and concisely. You can profile your receivers more tightly by asking yourself what is important to them and hit those points ASAP.

A quick story: Engineers from a pump manufacturer neglected the needs and wants of their audience by speaking about design and metallurgy to power plant operators who wanted to hear about operating cost and maintenance. The audience fidgeted and the presenters lost them and thousands of dollars.

To create logical progressions of thoughts, think cohesion/unity. Sentences, paragraphs, and entire documents are cohesive when they flow smoothly and clearly toward a defined conclusion or direction that is set by the purpose(s) of senders and receivers, establishing the parameters of your prose. The result is thoughts that are connected logically and clearly.

An editorial aside: Is communicating well out of favor? Is it needed? Many leaders feel, justifiably, that our society, including that venerable institution of business, has rejected the habit of and need for communicating well. Perhaps the main reason is our addiction to so many other media that have replaced good writing, led by the ease of voice communications via telephone, Skype, and voice-recognition software that translates our ramblings to text that is laden with grammatical and syntactical meanderings that our fifth-grade teachers would never condone. Then the computer and smart phones have blessed shorthand, now called texting, and emails that are 'good enough'. All have created the feeling, the conviction, that careful crafting of words is no longer necessary.

I t is, as demonstrated by firms that have lost contracts because of murky proposals and reports or been sued because of a muddy, ambiguous sentence in a proposal or contract … individuals who lost opportunities for employment because of an indecipherable resume, contested a murky last will and testament, lost a friend or client because of an insensitive email … and, for good measure, a very foggy Second Amendment to the US Constitution that has spurred endless political debates and struggles.

The negative consequences of communicating badly dig their destructive tentacles into our business, financial, and personal lives. The positive consequences of communicating well are as endemic.

Yes, people and companies are still hired because they can craft language that reflects intelligence, simply because, as pointed our earlier, many of us in this age of information sell nothing but our intelligence. Contracts are won because the proposal can be evaluated precisely, friendships are created because people find common ground via their language, lawsuits are avoided when contractual obligations are stated clearly, and jobs are landed by clear and persuasive resumes (have you thought of resumes as proposals? Or proposals as resumes?)

The benefits and impacts of good writing continue and extend well beyond transmitting information. Good writing *creates* information, and, therefore, good writing creates intelligence and literally forces that elusive human talent that we have labeled 'creativity'.

6. Continuous learning: The never-ending necessity with an impressive payback

"If you think education is expensive, try ignorance."
Derek Bok, former President, Harvard University.

It's easy to lose money in business: train your employees but neglect their other needs and watch them and their expensive intelligence walk out the door to greener pastures such as a competitor--ouch!--or to start their own company. While that's bad enough financially and psychically, to lose really big money don't train your employees and watch them stay with you. You can't afford that in this era when your only product is your intelligence.

Continuous learning, aka continuous improvement, is simply the process of continually improving skills and knowledge, in turn continually improving performance on the job and in all other parts of life. It can be thought of also as training tomorrow's leaders today, surely a integral part of sustainable competitive advantage. It can also be thought of as the best-- perhaps the only-- way to stay abreast of accelerating changes in technologies and management missions. Motivational speaker Zig Ziglar had the right idea when he said:" People often say that motivation (aka

training) doesn't last. Well, neither does bathing--
that's why we recommend it daily."

Organizations that have implemented continuous
improvement realize specific benefits in a clear chain
of events:

improved skills→ greater confidence→open, honest,
constructive communications without fear of
embarrassment → improved teamwork at all levels →
enhanced creativity and efficiency→ happiness,
fulfillment, and satisfaction→ higher revenue and
profit

Criteria for successful continuous learning include:

1. Clear, realistic objectives such as productivity
improvements and lower personnel turnover; begin
with the end in mind;

2. Precise alignment with the firm's and individuals'
mission, philosophy, core values, strategies, and
tactics: continuous learning is a strategic as well as
tactical initiative, and short-term benefits indicate
progress toward realizing longer-term goals and
encourage participants;

3. Continuous evaluation by attendees, sponsors, and
facilitators.

7. Critical/creative thinking: Another expression of intelligence

The definitions and inseparability of critical and creative thinking ...the five imperatives...spoofing the myth of sudden inspiration

"Innovation distinguishes between a leader and a follower." Steve Jobs

"To achieve success, first abandon popular delusions." Jerry, Porras, Stewart, Emery, and Mark Thompson in *Success Built to Last.*

Critical thinking is the process of assessing or judging thoughts expressed by drawings or documents with the aim of improving them. Engineers, scientists, and businesspersons tend to adhere intuitively to that process: they typically are critical thinkers; they are confident in their abilities to assess and figure out the logic of most technical and related issues, and they continually look for order, system, and relationships among concepts and thoughts--the essence of creativity.

Creative thinking—aka innovative, inventive, original, ingenious, resourceful, imaginative thinking-- is the process of making or producing that which has not been made or produced before. Even the simplest tasks in business demand ingenuity, insight, and judgment to evaluate the available options for overcoming a variety of technical and societal challenges.

Critical and creative thinking are intimately related: critical thinking is essential to define a need or problem, creative thinking to meet the need or solve a problem.

Businesspersons face a special paradox concerning critical and creative thinking: On one hand, their education--especially if they are technologists-- tends to focus on data collection and analysis, not on how to use the data in new ways to solve all sorts of problems and create all sorts of comforts for man. On the other hand, their everyday activities extend technology to the vital responsibility to improving man's condition in many facets of life, from aesthetics to a clean environment, fiduciary responsibility, and beyond.

The combination of critical and creative thinking can be defined further by what it is and isn't:

IT IS finding alternative solutions—solutions that are outside normal experience—to a situation/problem/human condition, bringing into being what was not there. The simple tab taught us a new way to open a beverage can—who remembers the church key that was once indispensible? Beethoven taught us that a symphony with a vocal movement is dramatic, Sony and Sirius and Apple taught us that music can be as mobile as we are, and GPS taught us that we don't need maps to know where we are and where we're going, and so on.

IT ISN'T the same old answers to the same old or similar new problems, which is what managers call stagnation, writers call block, and artists call a blank .*I've hit a brickwall … I can't get started …*and the latest: *It is what it is* and *It's the best I can do*--are omens of defeat that are guaranteed to sustain the status quo. Creativity is the spark of originality, of inspiration, of illumination that leads to new products and ground-breaking solutions.

The combination of critical and creative thinking isn't limited to so-called artistic types… advertisers, marketers, writers, painters, musicians and so on…they just get the publicity. Certainly we can agree that Mozart, Wagner, Stravinsky, Picasso, Shakespeare, Hemingway and others in a long list are creative because they found new ways to express the human condition. We can also agree that Tom

Watson, Bill Gates, Steve Jobs, Henry Ford, George Westinghouse, Thomas Edison, and Nicholas Tesla were and are just as creative in their own ways.

The single reason to be critical and creative is to help build sustainable competitive advantage for individuals, their employers/firms, and clients. For example, engineers must come up with new ideas every day; the more creative--aka innovative, inventive-- their ideas are, the better are their chances of being noticed by top managers and the better their chances for promotion, the better the odds that the firm will thrive well into the future, and the better the odds that their clients will thrive as well; everybody wins.

Becoming more critical and creative: The five imperatives (Paraphrased from The Foundation for Critical Thinking to be most germane to business)

1. Intellectual humility: willingness to distinguish what is known and unknown; openness to new concepts that overcomes intellectual arrogance.
2. Intellectual courage: willingness to challenge popular beliefs, practices, and standards while adhering to standards of rationality.

3. Intellectual curiosity: willingness to ask probing questions; to listen carefully to the ideas of others; to understand and either accept or reject outside ideas.

4. Careful listening to others, yourself, and especially your subconscious smarts, which releases you from all sorts of inhibitions that can prevent criticality and creativity. The brain is a wonderful device that allows incoming information to organize itself into patterns that are not necessarily logical or symmetrical or normal—but they are useful, and we use the patterns to give rise to creative solutions.

5. Clear and substantive writing, which exploits the disciplines of writing to discover what is known and unknown, important or unimportant.

Eschew the myth of sudden inspiration. It's rare

The upward trajectory of your career and the sustainability of your firm depend to a great extent on coming up with great ideas, and you can't rely on chance to make that happen.

Dr. Edward Land, the inventor of the Polaroid camera, misled his audience when he defined creativity as, "The sudden cessation of stupidity." Perhaps Dr. Land was influenced by Archimedes, the Greek mathematician and inventor who, around 250 BCE, supposedly leaped from his bathtub and announced that he had discovered how to determine the volume and composition of an irregular shape by shouting *Eureka*—Greek for 'I found it'. He implied that his discovery was an epiphany that appeared suddenly and without prior knowledge or planning. Actually, it was the result of years of study.

The myth of inspiration lives on, but the reality of the matter is that critical and creative thinking are accessible to all human beings who can think and are fully engaged in their work and life, and who take systematic and deliberate steps that are far more likely to deliver creative solutions than is inspiration:

1. Define your purpose clearly and precisely;
2. Brainstorm with others or yourself (brainstorming does not require group interaction) to identify many ways, feasible or not, to meet your purpose, then selecting the few that best do so;
3. Examine the data and assumptions that can support the purpose and the best ways to meet it;
4. Understand the positive and negative implications and consequences that emanate from steps one through three;
5. Decide on a course of action, and then examine it to be certain that it meets, or will meet, your purpose as stated in Step 1.

Creativity, according to artists, psychologists, and scholars, originates in the unconscious, often when the mind is not specifically engaged in completing a task or solving a problem. For example, Einstein's theory of relativity came to him while he was dozing, Descartes conceived his rationalistic theory while in the midst of a dream, and jack Nicklaus reportedly came up with a new golf grip while asleep. These creative geniuses, and countless others, were thinking about the subject by:

1. Preparing: collecting, researching, reading, thinking, and letting their minds wander;

2. Incubating: letting their minds--typically their unconscious minds-- reorganize and elaborate on the material collected;

3. Illuminating: understanding thoughts within the context if an experience, intuition, insight, hunch, a feeling of correctness; and

4. Verifying: finding the necessary proof of correctness.

Enhance creativity by eschewing these common inhibitors:

We know what we need to do, but don't know how to do it: Follow the four steps above.

My well is dry: Listen to your unconscious mind, your dreams (the direct path to your unconscious), and turn that dry well into a fountain of creativity.

I don't have time: The most productive and creative people are the busiest, a truism that is supported by that old saw: "if you want something done, give it to a busy person and it will be done." Why? Busy persons manage their time more efficiently and flexibly; they tend to awaken and immediately focus on the tasks ahead; they put aside or delegate mundane tasks such as getting the car washed. Time is more of an excuse than a reason.

8. Fallacies of logic: The expressions of ignorance to avoid

Red herrings, non-sequiturs, overblown generalizations and other fallacies destroy logic and careers

"When you stop chasing the wrong things, you give the right things a chance to catch you." Lolly Daskal, founder of *Lead From Within*, a global consultancy.

Fallacies are flawed arguments--blips or shortcomings in critical thinking-- that discerning readers and listeners will recognize and conclude that the writer or speaker is chasing the wrong things, is not too bright or, worse, is dishonest, just what leaders want to avoid. The first step in avoiding most or all is to understand what they are:

A. NON-SEQUITUR, also called *red herring*, or *it doesn't follow* occurs when a communicator changes the subject to distract receivers from the issue at hand, typically in two parts of a sentence or two adjoining sentences. Consider this sentence intended to justify high prices: "The company may charge high prices, but it gives a great deal of money to charity." Perhaps that sentence might read: "The company may seem to charge high prices, but its products are superior to others' in many ways."

B.UNSUPPORTED/OVERBLOWN GENERALIZATION is a sweeping statement that is not supported by evidence and can be a topic sentence of a paragraph or a head or subhead. *Everyone should exercise* does not allow for exceptions such as the bedridden or otherwise incapable. Is *everyone who can should exercise* better? Or *Many people benefit from regular exercise. Most people benefit from regular exercise?* (Is *most* too close to absolute?)

You can spot unsupported generalizations by such absolute words as *always, never, all, everyone, best, most* (in its superlative sense but not in its quantitative sense) and others of similar superlative ilk.

C.CONFUSING CAUSE AND EFFECT which logicians call *ad hoc* reasoning. In other words, "Because B happened after A, A caused B." Proving cause and effect can be difficult and can be confused with *correlation,* a far weaker relationship.

A consultant reports: *ABC is the most responsive to customers' needs.* Is that supportable?

An infamous example: Stock market indices rise and fall with the rise and fall of the Ganges River (or ladies' dress hemlines.)

D. THE EXPERIENCE/HISTORY TRAP—a form of confusing cause and effect--confuses experience with expertise when the *results* of experience and expertise are the real point. In other words, *what* you or your firm has done is less important than *why* you did it and *how* it benefitted your client. An infamous example:

Experience … We have worked with the finest companies—from the Fortune 500 to leading local firms. Whatever your company size or service need, ABC will provide prompt, accurate, quality and cost-effective services.

Finest? Leading? The two thoughts are out of balance, a form of out of parallel. The second sentence does not follow the first, a non sequitur.

E. EQUIVOCATION, a shift in the meaning of data or a key word:

From an engineer's report: ABC's proposed gas conditioning system consists of a single train, two vessel, 304 stainless steel selective regenerable adsorption systems.

How many systems?

From thePittsburgh Post Gazette: It is no secret that the Pittsburgh region is an area of slow growth.

Is Pittsburgh a region or an area? (And, BTW, equivocation generally leads to wordiness. This thought can be expressed more concisely: It's obvious that the Pittsburgh region is growing slowly.)

From a consultant's qualification statement: ABC is a nationwide firm that has been providing quality geotechnical engineering services and drilling, construction testing and inspection, and environmental consulting services for more than 100 years.

How many services?

Another consultant writes: ABC consultants was able to assist CUSTOMER in solving numerous on site problems such as underground utilities, slope stabilization, and building construction problems.

How many problems? And, are underground utilities problems? (only if they are mal-functioning.)

F. SOLIPSISM, the view that the self is all that exists or is known; writing for yourself and not receivers; aka **narcissism**, excessive interest in oneself.

G. HYPERBOLE: An exaggerated statement that is not meant to be taken literally, but often is and then becomes bragging and can be confused with unsupported generalization.

A consultant writes: Our commitment to value and quality is unparalleled in the industry. (Totally unsupportable, impossible to prove or demonstrate.)

An editorial aside concerning thinking: We would like to see a world in which fair-minded critical thinking becomes a broad social value, where it is truly encouraged throughout education and all other institutions, especially business where it can be most visible and most needed. We are a long way from that ideal. According to research conducted from around 1960 to 2014, and as reported by The Critical Thinking Foundation, "very little critical thinking occurs at any level of the college or university in the U.S. today (I2014). The seminal Roska study (Academically Adrift, 2011) " ... mirrors (the Foundation's)1997 state-wide study for the California

Commission on Teacher Credentialing ... public and private colleges and universities believe critical thinking to be of primary importance to instruction (89%), relatively few can articulate a reasonable conception of it (19%), and only 9% teach critical thinking on a typical class day."

PART III:
RESPONSIBLE BEHAVIORS THAT PUT THINKING INTO ACTION

"A man cannot be separated from his mind; his life cannot be separated from his thoughts. Mind, thought and life are as inseparable as light, radiance and color ...it follows that to deliberately change the thoughts is to change the man." James Allen, British philosopher, 1864-1912, a pioneer in self-help and author of the influential book, *As a man Thinketh.*

9. Problem analyses/decision-making: Gut reactions can fall short

Intuition can benefit from disciplined thinking...the steps toward better, more constructive decisions

To solve a problem it is necessary to think. It is necessary to think even to decide what facts to collect." Robert Maynard Hutchins, 1899-1977, American educational philosopher and former President, University of Chicago.

Problem analyses and decision-making are intuitive, the result of experience in the trenches, right? Maybe that's true for some leaders, but probably not all, and, likely, all can benefit from diligent, persistent, and disciplined thinking that defines precisely what is wrong (the problem), how things got that way, and the most economical and effective way(s) to correct the problem. It extends far beyond such techniques as brainstorming. A suggested procedure:

A. Recognize the problem: A problem is nothing more or less than a deviation from some standard of performance--of what *should be*-- that has been set by someone, e.g. par on a golf course set by the PGA, sales quotas set by sales managers, earnings per share set by the board of directors and /or stock analysts, and so on. The standard of performance is a measure against which actual performance can be gauged. Two conditions--often related-- must exist before a deviation becomes a problem: the leader must recognize that the deviation is undesirable, and the leader must identify its cause and remove it. Only then can the leader move to ...

B. Identify and rank the objectives and actions for resolving the problem: The overall objective for resolving any problem is to revert deviations from norm to the planned norm. Specifically, every problem comes with its own set of objectives and resolutions. For example, When Bill O'Rourke arrived in Russia to lead Alcoa's largest plant to profitability, the overall objective, he was confronted with a plethora of conditions/problems that tended to thwart any progress toward meeting that objective. Among them was the worst safety record--a huge and unpalatable deviation-- among all of Alcoa's plants, and he decided that removing that deviation was his top priority. Others, at almost the same level of priority and implemented concurrently, were reducing the workforce in ways that met Alcoa's (decidedly not Russia's) severance policies, and replacing a culture of animosity and corruption with one of cooperation and honesty. The plant was profitable in only two years. (You can read about Bill's experiences in *The Power of Ethics,* a book he co-authored with Pete Geissler.)

C. Consider future consequences, including the unintended: Nobody can predict the future with absolute certainty. To verify that statement and enjoy a few laugh-out-loud moments, visit *bad predictions* on the Internet, and ask yourself: If we can predict the future, why are there traffic jams? Rain on your picnic? Why are there losers at the race tracks? The stock exchange?

Nevertheless and despite our shortcomings, we cannot live without trying to predict, whether the events in our day (which sounds simple, but how many times have your plans been disrupted by unanticipated or unintended events?); or visualizing the future many years down the road. The divorce rate, now at 55% for first marriages, is a common failure in visualizing the future; very few people anticipate divorce when they marry.

In business, we can be quite certain that the top managers at GM did not anticipate that an ignition switch would cause fires, massive recalls, and restructuring of the company to focus , at least publicly, on safety. Nor did the top managers at Westinghouse anticipate the real estate crisis that literally destroyed the company's balance sheet and eventually bankrupted it.

The law of unintended consequences rears its ugly, manic-depressive head when least expected.

Sociologist Robert K. Merton popularized the law of unintended consequences (The Law, hereafter) in his 1936 paper, *The Unanticipated Consequences of Purposive Social Action*. In it, Merton attempted to systematically analyze the problem of unintended consequences of deliberate acts intended to cause social change.

More recently, The Law has come to be a warning that intervention in a complex situation tends to create unanticipated consequences that can be:

- Positive, an unexpected benefit usually attributed to good fortune or luck (which can be tricky since there is some truth in the aphorisms that luck favors the wise and the prepared);
- Negative, an unexpected detriment in addition to the positive benefit, usually attributed to bad luck or fortune; and/or

- Perverse, contrary to the original intent; when the intended consequence worsens the outcome, usually attributed to stupidity or ignorance.

Violations of the law are perpetrated by the arrogance of leaders or individuals such as sports icons--Tiger Woods and Tom Brady leap immediately to mind but there are many others--who believe that they can accurately predict future consequences (nobody can), and/or they believe that any consequences will be ignored or even accepted by others (possible, but not certain). Other causes might be *ignorance* based on incomplete analysis; *honest error* based on incorrect analysis; and *short-sightedness* that is typically based on immediate, egocentric interests that ignore the longer term.

The impacts of The Law are palpable and numerous: For example, on the side of positive consequences, aspirin was found to have beneficial health effects beyond relieving pain; negative: prohibition led to more bars and more drinking as citizens rebelled; and perverse: the automobile has increased mobility but also air pollution, millions of accidental deaths and injuries, and loss of wildlife habitats.

10. The universal need for ethics: Business is the perfect catalyst

Universal definitions the need for a more ethical society...examples of ethical and unethical behavior and their impacts

"I believe, indeed, that overemphasis on the purely intellectual att., often directed solely to the practical and factual, in our education, has led directly to the impairment of ethical values.' Albert Einstein

Most--dare we say all?— professions such as engineering, law, and journalism; institutions such as government, education, and sports; and groups of people with similar interests such as Hell's Angels and companies—have adopted codes of ethics to guide, limit, restrict, and generally define expected behavior of all their members. The codes generally state that the member should 'do what's right.' The problem is that different people perceive different behavior to be 'right' at different times; more explanation is essential if the codes are to be meaningful and enforceable.

The issue of ethics is universal. All people face ethical situations in their professional and personal lives: conflicts of interest, suspicion of wrongdoing, dishonesty, theft, misrepresentation (aka lying, mis-speaking, and spinning the truth), and downright chicanery and cheating, aka self-serving reasoning and the destructive actions it causes.

Business ethics refers to standards of conduct that, in an ideal world, every stakeholder--shareholders, employees, customers, suppliers, community residents and so on--- wants and is expected to follow. It includes the notion that the person, the single entity of a business, and the far broader institution of business itself requires that members have and display a certain degree of competence before acting in a manner where others will be relying on that competence. Engineering ethics, for example, assures the public that it can rely on the technical actions or assertions of the engineer and that the result will meet the intended or represented specifications, that, for example, the bridge will not fall and the machine will operate as promised. Journalism ethics demands that the information reported be true and, in many cases, original in the sense that it is not plagiarized.

Most codes of ethics offer assurances of health, safety, reliability, environmental sustainability, quality, durability, and economy by way of fiscal responsibility--plus other desirable traits of products, services, and behaviors. Yet, many of these concepts involve trade-offs such as planned obsolescence, cost/benefit analysis, and risk management. Nobody can guarantee 100% fitness for use, precise financial statements, impeccable product quality, or absolute personnel safety, for example, but everybody can adhere to generally accepted standards so that the public understands exactly what is being represented, warranted, and assured.

Many firms, regardless of size or type, have adopted 'Values' (almost all including 'Integrity'), and their own codes of conduct. Many have appointed Chief Compliance Officers for ethics, just as they have appointed compliance officers for law, safety, health, environmental responsibility, fiscal control, and sustainability. Some companies have created networks of Integrity Champions comprised of respected and trusted individuals who can be consulted when difficult issues arise. All employees from janitors to directors are expected to behave in accordance with those corporate values.

The core of ethical behavior is personal integrity. Individuals make choices, right or wrong, good or bad, ethical or unethical. Those choices are inevitably reflected in the organization or institution where they work.

Business--or any organization, for that matter-- is challenged continuously to do what is right. However, the mandate for meeting ever-rising annual and quarterly expectations for profitability, the stress of time and creativity in the workplace, the drive to complete every task better, faster, and cheaper, often with limited funds-- doing what is 'right' is not always the easy choice. Still, it is always the best choice, the only choice. When Vince Lombardi—that icon of unbending and demanding leadership in the business of sports-- famously said that 'winning is everything', he meant that winning is his and his team's only choice. We hope that he added: 'within the rules of the game'.

Six steps to ethical power: It's not difficult or mysterious

Businesses and the jobs they create will be more sustainable and profitable if all employees—including and especially top executives -- behave ethically at all times; directors should be included, but they are typically so distant from operations that it is futile to expect them to be integral parts of the organization.

The point is that ethics is a full-time job that permeates all disciplines. To that end, leaders must equip all employees with the formal, six-step process needed to clearly identify, understand, and successfully resolve ethical dilemmas.

Step One: Recognize: If a situation creates feelings of unease or queasiness there may be an ethical dilemma that needs to be resolved. Even before proceeding to the ethical reasoning strategy outlined below, please consider the insights of modern moral psychology and neuroscience; they suggest that emotional reactions are rational and relevant to moral reasoning. Unconscious perception of ethical or moral dissonance, when it bubbles up to the surface of our awareness, deserves full attention.

Caution: While knee-jerk, gut reactions might alert you to a potential issue, acting solely on such signals may be irresponsible. In fact, research has demonstrated that blindly following one's intuition can result in less-than-optimal outcomes; therefore, please complement intuition with a robust, intentional, and deliberative strategy for identifying and resolving ethical dilemmas.

This first step assumes that the person taking it has the ethical maturity needed to discern ethical from unethical, right from wrong. We call on Aristotle for a description of ethical persons/judges, and we paraphrase and interpret:

Ethical persons, and those that judge the ethics of other persons, possess the admirable human characteristics that fit a person for life in an organized civic community, and considers how such characteristics can be fostered or created and their opposites prevented.

Consider that many people do not appreciate or recognize ethical dilemmas, and that the best teacher of recognition is experience.

Busy-ness is not an excuse for failing to recognize an ethics issue; it is not a reason to de-activate ourethical filters. Everyone is busy, some of us too busy, with long to-do lists and seemingly impossible deadlines imposed by demanding bosses and family pressures. Tip: think of overwhelming busy-ness as an opportunity to pause and reflect.

Step Two: Research: Only after examining the situation--most have more than two points of view, especially when the ethical issue is unclear--and gathering the relevant facts can leaders begin to understand and articulate the precise dynamics of the issue. This step can help or hinder any resolution: It helps if the perceived ethical dilemma can be mitigated or completely resolved early and quickly, as gathering and clarifying relevant facts may reveal an inconsequential misunderstanding or missing information. It can hinder if gathering and clarifying the facts can confirm, complicate, and intensify an ethics dilemma by adding a dispute regarding the facts.

The bottom line: Commit to ascertaining as much information as possible--delegate fact-finding to a trusted associate if necessary-- so that your analysis is not compromised by erroneous assumptions and blind spots and can be defended against the deepest scrutiny by third parties and the public. But move as quickly as practicable; delay can be construed as condoning the behavior in question.

Step 3: Repose: Stop, pause, and engage in circumspect and creative contemplation to discern various options for acting within a given situation and to envision the potential help and harm that are likely to result. Only then can future regrets and confrontations caused by failure to recognize and consider a full range of possible actions be avoided.

Step 4. Reconcile: Questioning the realities and consequences of options and relating them to what's right and wrong will clarify the values and priorities implicit in ultimate decisions. Interrogations might be guided by examining:

IMPACTS ON OTHERS:

--Who are all the stakeholders that will be impacted by this option, and how will they be impacted? In other words, what are the foreseeable consequences of your decision on people, profits, and the planet? Does this option create shared value or will it result in a zero sum outcome?

 --Does this option result in the least amount of foreseeable suffering? If harm is inevitable, does this option fairly and efficiently allocate benefits and burdens to all impacted parties?

--Are human rights, rules/regulations of your profession, corporate/organizational codes of conduct, or any U.S./international laws implicated by your decision? Is there a law, principle, or policy that simply must be followed or enforced? If so, you might be legally obligated to report the incident and its resolution.

IMPACTS ON YOURSELF:

--What duties or responsibilities do you owe to stakeholders? Do you owe a special duty to your company and/or its investors?

--Would you prefer this option if you were adversely impacted by it?

--How would you feel if everyone selected this option in a similar situation? Is this option in harmony with your organization's culture and norms?

--What type of person might you become if you choose this option and ones similar to it on a continuing basis? For instance, if you want to be known as a reliable and responsible person, what would this option say about your character and integrity?

--Will you be able to look at yourself in the mirror and be comfortable with the person you see and put your head on the pillow and sleep well at night if you choose this option? What type of legacy are you creating for yourself and your organization?

--Could you defend your actions before shareholders, the Board of Directors, peers, and family?

--How would you look if this situation was completely transparent--if the facts were interpreted and reported on the front page of the *New York Times*, *Wall Street Journal,* or your local paper? Or on national or local TV news? Or on Twitter or Face book? How would your Mother react?

Step 5. Respond: Select and implement the option that survives the rigorous investigation completed in Step 4 as the best and most rational in the sense that it minimizes impacts on others and yourself, maximizes expectations of integrity and honesty, and is consistent with your values and virtues. Be prepared to defend your choice; you may be pressed for a more rigorous explanation by others who disagree with or question your decision. If someone else is responsible for acting, recommend actions and follow up to be sure that your recommendations are considered fully and fairly. Not acting is not an option: it condones unethical behavior and sends the wrong signal to everyone in the entire organization, many of whom will be watching.

Step 6: Review. Only then can you continuously improve the process and the ethical behavior of employees and image of your organization. Ask yourself:

--Was publicity appropriate?

--Did the punishment fit the crime?

--Could the situation have been avoided with pre-emptive steps? Can you change/improve the culture/structure of your organization so that similar issues can be avoided or made less vexing in the future?

--Could you have completed the investigation more quickly, thoroughly, and fairly?

--Could you be better prepared if confronted by a similar situation in the future? Could you assure others and yourself that this situation can never be repeated?

11. Dignity: Basic to a civil society

Treating people with dignity and respect lead inevitably leads to long-term success...the critical role of safety... examples...a proposal for universal acceptance

"The superior man understands what is right; the inferior man understands what will sell." Confucius

Where is the dignity unless there is honesty? *Cicero, Roman philosopher, 106BCE--43BCE*

Employees, customers, and other stakeholders are far more than every business's most important assets; they are the source of all other assets. Treat them with the dignity they deserve and prosper financially and socially.

Much has been written about the importance of people within and around any business. But, it seems, nobody has explained their importance as the sources of all other assets despite its universal truth. Yet many firms demean their sources assets and it has hurt and destroyed many lives. Classic examples include ENRON, TYCO, Adelphia, Westinghouse, Dravo, and many others.

The root cause of many failures—and the corrosive, corrupting force that destroys dignity—is that familiar goblin: managing for stockholder value, or an incessant drive for profitable growth, which is a euphemism for the same misguided mission of management. Many actually consider managing for stockholder value to be amoral and a cruel hoax, and that too many self-serving, short-sighted and, as a consequence, destructive decisions are made in its name. This conviction is tackled by Jack Markowitz, an esteemed business editor at *The Pittsburgh Tribune Review*. He wrote in his column of July 25, 2013, that: "CEO pay, perks and stock options have inflated so wildly that rank and file workers have to grind their teeth at the unshared sacrifice of keeping companies competitive."

Nevertheless, managing for stockholder value and dignity can be compatible goals or drivers of policy—they can live together in peace and harmony, but it is rare. One example: Paul O'Neill of International Paper and Alcoa. His guiding principle was the safety of all employees, other stakeholders, customers who buy and use Alcoa 's products, and the public at large, which translates nicely to caring for their well-being, a big part of dignity and ethics.

During Mr. O'Neill's tenure at Alcoa, the accident rate throughout the company plummeted and the stock price soared, demonstrating that managing for stockholder value and the soft side can live together harmoniously.

Early in 2004 The Harvard Business School agreed tacitly that managing for stockholder value is amoral: it started a semester-long course in ethics for its MBA students. In announcing the course, the dean said, reportedly with a shocked expression as if this revelation was brand new: "An unsettling number of business leaders apparently have put their own motives and profit before integrity." The University of Maryland has taken a different approach to the same subject; its business students tour prisons and interview white-collar criminals in an effort to scare them—the students, not the inmates—into some sense of integrity.

Perhaps not so strangely, the chairman of a giant manufacturer of electronic equipment said, after his predecessor's attempts at managing for stockholder value had failed and the stock price of his company dropped more than eighty percent, that "stock price is a byproduct (of good management); stock price isn't a driver. And any time I've seen any of us (presumably top managers) lose sight of that, it has always been a painful experience." I wonder if he feels the pain of the thousands of smaller investors who lost their shirts before he came to this revelation.

Strange, isn't it that the stakeholders that must be classified as big losers to the mission of stockholder value are the millions of smaller stockholders who were supposed to benefit. Other big losers are the towns and cities in which these companies operated, and all the local support businesses and their employees...customers who were forced to find other suppliers...employees who were forced to find other jobs and careers.

A former top executive at Westinghouse (one of the very good managers who was fired/retired because he tried to infuse some integrity into the company) wondered rhetorically how many millions of lives were disrupted or ruined because of the company's—management's—failure...how many divorces, lost college educations, postponed or cancelled retirements, resulted. He could think of hundreds. Millions of personal trials and disasters is not hype by any means, and this from one of the smaller and less-publicized incidents, and perhaps one that showed the way for others.

12. RESULTS HR: Minimize experience, maximize value

Experience is less important than results that add value...the most important questions in hiring ...evaluating resumes

'...the biggest differentiator between an average company and a great company is the motivation of the people within the company ..." Chip Conley, founder and CEO, Joie de Vive Hospitality and author of PEAK and other books.

Leaders tend to be pretty confident – except when it comes to hiring.

In 2011, a leadership and training company called Leadership IQ published the findings of a three-year study on the effectiveness of interviewing techniques. The consulting firm had followed 20,000 hiring decisions made by 5,247 hiring managers in 312 public and private organizations.

The results? Only 19% of all new hires could be considered unequivocal successes. Forty-six percent of all new hires fail within the first 18 months on the job. That's right; for most companies, the reliability of their hiring practices is not much better than flipping a coin.

But here's the really interesting thing: Of the group of failures, only 11% were terminated because they lacked the required technical competence. The vast majority were not successful because, in one way or another, they were personally unsuited for the job. Maybe they didn't have the right interpersonal capabilities, or they weren't motivated to do the job the way the business needs it done, or they couldn't change course when someone told them things weren't working out.

So often, these people's exits are followed by small groups of former co-workers or managers who offer their post-mortems around the water cooler. "Bob just couldn't make Acme happy, and they're our toughest client," they'll offer with pitying head shakes. Or maybe, "Steve was too focused on the details, and that job really needs someone who can step into a leadership role." Those are often perfectly valid statements.

Every hirer's one critical question: ignore it at your peril

The real key to making better hiring decisions is to ask one question. It's not for the candidate to answer in the interview, though; it's for the hirer to answer, and before filling out the job requisition.

"What are the three to five value-added accomplishments this person must deliver in the first 12 months on the job?"

Every job has three components –qualifications, duties, and deliverables.

Most hiring decisions start and stop by defining needs as qualifications, like, "a BS in Civil Engineering and five years' experience in the natural gas industry." Defining requirements solely in terms of broad qualifications will generate a hefty stack of unsuitable resumes, while providing little guidance as to how to evaluate them.

The how-to-do-HR books will tell you that good hiring starts with an accurate job description. It doesn't. Besides qualifications and language for legal compliance, job descriptions mostly describe duties. Sure, you need to be clear on what a person is supposed to do in a job, but that's not enough. Duties rarely change much year over year, but priorities do, especially as you go higher in the organization.

For example: This year a procedure manual needs to be rewritten; next year, it could be a new product or service that needs to be developed. And very often, such varied priorities exist in two jobs with exactly identical job descriptions. Those priorities aren't duties, they're deliverables that can be held your hand, seen on the ground or on a computer screen, or found on the bottom line. Hiring teams tend to sit down with candidates having no shared understanding of what the deliverables for a job are – at least until the new hire fails to deliver them.

Focus on value-added deliverables. Begin with the ending in mind

There are deliverables, and there are deliverables. Be sure that your interview process assesses a candidate's capability to deliver results that are truly value-added, as opposed to those that are non-value-added. A value-added deliverable is one that the end user – a customer, a client, or the boss – is willing to pay for; it's that thing he or she is really buying. It could be the same as a non-value-added deliverable, but it may not be. For example, a senior engineering position may list "prepares client reports" as a duty on its job description. The deliverable, of course, would be a completed client report.

But is that really the value-added deliverable? Chances are the client doesn't really want to pay for a report; he really wants to buy a recommendation about what he should be doing to fix a problem and what he should stop doing that's making the problem worse. There's the value-added deliverable, and a candidate's ability to provide it needs to be assessed during the interview.

Assessing what a person has done isn't the same as digging into what a person has delivered. There is preparing client reports, and there is delivering a well-researched, thoroughly analyzed, professionally presented recommendation that offers the client a substantial perceived value. And there is that one-off need like researching foreign government regulations to support a client's overseas operations that you really must have in the next 10 months, but won't write about on the job description.

Hirers need deeper insights into real, value-added needs

Clarifying the value-added deliverables provides the interviewer with a deeper insight into the real needs, and thus makes clear what the interview questions should be. Skip those over-broad questions like, "how would you describe your management style?"

for which all candidates have the same canned answer ("Tough but fair:" Aren't we all?) and get to the ones that tell you what you really need, like "tell me about your best success with developing a young, inexperienced team into a successful one."

List those three to five accomplishments in a SMART format, meaning each one should be specific (deals with one thing), measurable (provides a way of ensuring it's done), achievable (doable given the resources at hand), relevant (to the job or larger organization's goals), and time-bound (has a deadline). Here are some examples:

- Acquire at least one new client in the natural gas industry within 12 months.
- Achieve company compliance with state regulation 12345 by year end.
- Ensure the group's ability to use XYZ equipment within seven months.

The experience trap; avoid it or pay dearly

Defining hiring needs in terms of years of experience is common, and it is helpful, especially for applicants; but to stop the needs analysis there is a mistake. Employment lawyers love experience requirements because they can defend them in court to a jury, and many interviewers think they're an efficient shorthand for gauging a person's capability; but in the real world, people of similar years' experience in similar backgrounds can have such different accomplishments and talents that using time as your yardstick is really pretty lazy.

Besides, the talent pool is overflowing with long-tenured mediocrities. The fact that someone has done something a lot does not mean he's done it well.

A list of qualifications has its place in the hiring process. So does a job description. But the first and most valuable step is to define the necessary value-added accomplishments needed in the next year. You don't make a great hiring decision based on what a person has. Neither will you make it based on listing what a person has to do. The best hiring decisions start with knowing what a person has to deliver.

13. Entrepreneurship and intraneurship: Leaders want more, but?

The differences and the common benefits...essential personality traits.. Why leaders encourage them

"A real entrepreneur is somebody who has no safety net." Henry Kravis

An entrepreneur is an owner/manager who takes full responsibility for a business--typically a smaller, stand-alone business-- and is willing to pay the price for failures and reap the rewards for successes. An intrapreneur is an entrepreneur within a larger organization, typically a manager of a department or business unit that reports to a higher authority.

Entrepreneurs and intrapreneurs are:

- Initiators: willing to champion actions to which competitors can respond; be first to introduce new products and services;

- Risk takers: willing to take on projects with a high risk of failure and superior returns; to be aggressive in pursuing new opportunities; to not allow the fear of losing be greater than the excitement of winning;

- Innovators: willing to focus funds and other assets on research and development of new and improved products, services, and technologies.

Leaders in larger organizations prize these three traits so highly that they are often taught as part of continuous learning, as they should be. They are also prized and encouraged by governments interested in creating jobs: some 80 percent of new jobs are created by smaller organizations and start-ups. They also are prized--or should be prized--by enlightened employees of larger organizations who are concerned with:

- Security: Being an intrapreneur prepares many employees for the next step in their careers: entrepreneurship. More than one in six employees who leave their jobs for any reason start their own businesses.

- Success: Intrapreneurism can lead to rapid advancement and recognition in supportive organizations. For example, many, if not most., of *Fortune* 500 companies have engaged in intrapreneurial activities, often called *venturing*, in order to grow revenue and profit via new product lines. Those employees who venture are often promoted above those who don't.

14. Public virtue: Business can lead the way

The roots in the Founding Fathers...its prevalence today...its financial, societal, and psychic benefits

Our Founding Fathers somehow knew that public virtue was *"the real welfare of the great body of people ...it is the supreme object to be pursued."* Herbert Hoover followed: *"American business needs a lifting purpose greater than the struggle of materialism."* He was referring to public virtue, often cloaked as community support.

Today, it's easy to believe that public virtue has succumbed to individual greed and corporate malfeasance simply by perusing the newspaper headlines, TV sound bites and so-called talk shows, and Internet rants.

Public virtue is alive and, if not as well as it could be, surely it isn't among the living dead. In fact, the common good and private gain are compatible bedfellows in many companies--one top leader says in more than 90% of them--but we'll never know for sure.

Suffice it to say that many successful companies of all sizes and types believe in a and practice public virtue.

In fact, One desirable attribute of employees pinpointed by employers in a survey conducted by The National Association of Colleges and Employers was "has done volunteer work".

Further evidence can be found in Christine Arena's book, *Cause for Success.* In it, she describes in detail "How solving the world's problems improves corporate health, growth, and competitive edge." One sentence speaks volumes: "The company's (in this case, Eziba's) actions have also created business results ranging from supply chain efficiency to new streams of income, increased employee morale, and a distinct competitive edge."

Many other examples can be found in *Success Built to Last,* about which Jack Canfield, bestselling author of *Chicken Soup for the Soul,* said "If we are to create a world that works for everyone, we must create lives that matter."

One of the many universal traits of leadership is magnanimity--nobly generous, not only of money, but also of time and intellect. Perhaps magnanimity is most clearly demonstrated by the many corporate foundations that support the arts in so many communities, The Gates Foundation is one of the more visible. Bill O'Rourke, one of the contributors to this book, sat on the board of The Alcoa Foundation and helped to recommend donations to many groups that support communities worldwide.

A perfect example of public virtue: The Pittsburgh Symphony was saved from bankruptcy by a large grant from the former CEO of a major steel producer ...and a ten percent cut in salary by the several hundred musicians and administrators. All knew that the symphony is a valuable community asset for its concerts, outreach educational programs, and global ambassadorship for the city and the United States.

P.T. Barnum, 1810-1891, was right when he said: "Money-getters are the benefactors of our race. To them ... are we indebted to our institutions of learning, and of art, our academies, colleges, and churches."

The list is endless.

PART IV:
LASTING RELATIONSHIPS VIA FOCUSED MARKETING

When Calvin Coolidge famously said that *"everyone is selling something"*, he set off a raft of imitators including this by Jay Abraham: *"The fact is that everyone is in sales. Whatever area you work in, you do have clients and you do need to sell."*

Calvin and Jay were really talking about marketing, a far broader concept than sales.

Marketing is an essential part of The Human Side: It is the most public expression of the intelligence of individuals and firms; therefore, it is the ultimate differentiator and creator of sustainable competitive advantage.

15. What's so mysterious about marketing?: The confusion continues

Defining marketing and marketing communications by their by traits and results...examples

Marketing **is** the activity or process involving research, promotion, sales, and distribution of a product or service.

Regis McKenna, who made millions teaching Silicon Valley how to market computers and their brethren, became famous for marketing the idea that marketing is everything a company does, even accounting and legal. He's correct.

Peter Drucker expanded: the purpose of a business is to create a customer. If the purpose of a business is to create a customer, and marketing is everything a business does, then the purpose of marketing is to create and then keep that customer for repeat business. 'Keep' is at least as important as 'create' simply because 'create' costs 10 to 50 times more than 'keep'.

Ergo, marketing is everything a business does to create and keep customers---sales, distribution, operations, project management, engineering, letters, emails, brochures, ads—you name it.

Marketing is also defined by its essential traits. It is…

A. Strategic, long term—not a one-shot activity. Sales is about booking the contract now being negotiated, while marketing is about booking the contract that will be negotiated in the future.

B. Demanding of a plan and a commitment of funds and people that overrides swings in business. Marketing has persistent and courageous advocates.

C. Complementary and cooperative. All functions in the organization must buy into the goal of creating and keeping customers. Perhaps the most important marketers in many companies are project engineers and managers; they tend to be closest to customers for longer periods; they can make or break current and future contracts.

Marketing communications is a big and very visible and public part of marketing, and can also be defined in several ways:

A. Its products--ads, brochures, speeches, letters, direct mail, email, web sites, and so on. If marketing is everything, then marketing communications is all the written and oral communications to all your many audiences-- customers, stockholders, suppliers, government officials, and so on.

B. Its influence on those who read and hear about your products. Your audiences are harsh---they judge you and your organization by your marketing communications. Sloppy wording equals a sloppy writer, speaker, and entire organization. Incoherent, wordy, illogical messages paint senders with the same traits. Avoid them.

C. Its production process. Marketing communications can be defined by the process of producing them: conceive, write, design, print/record/present, distribute, evaluate, revise, repeat.

D. Its purposes or functions. The broad purpose marketing communications is to persuade, which includes such tasks enhancing images, supporting sales, and helping senders decide what exactly they are selling. Yes, the process of producing marketing communications will, in fact, help senders define what their business is all about, but only if they adhere to the disciplines of writing.

E. Its content. Basically, all marketing communications cover three points, preferably in this order:

--Why the receivers should buy what the senders are marketing—your position, unique selling/marketing proposition. All sellers have one, even if they are selling a commodity, and finding the USP/UMP is often the most difficult task of marketing and marketing communications, the reason it is ignored too often. See below for tips.

--What senders offer, in specific terms. The broad terms 'engineering', a 'circuit breaker', a 'building', are meaningless to receivers; the specific phrases 'engineering for efficient and green buildings', 'circuit breakers that optimize safety', a building that is more attractive to renters' are more specific and persuasive. Then ask yourself—am I marketing what the customer wants? How well do I know my customers?

--Who will do the work, and their credentials and credibility as defined by the results of their experience and expertise, often supported by publications and honors.

16. Techniques for influencing: They're the backbone of marketing

The singular purpose of all business communications is to influence behavior and thinking...here's how

It bears repeating: The purpose of every marketing communication in business is to influence—to create a desired effect, impression, or impact—on receivers of messages, whether they are readers or listeners. The desired effect may be to buy a product, to think highly of a person's skills and organization, bestow an award, and so on. To be most influential, consider an individual's or firm's:

Image/credibility: Receivers will be more likely to be influenced by senders they think of as like themselves than they think of as different. Engineers are hired to sell to engineers, writers to teach writing, and so on.

Opening line: The influence of a marketing message is increased dramatically if it opens with views shared by readers. Thus, a mayor's proposal for a new bridge might open with a statement that traffic will be alleviated for all.

Closing lines: In general, explicit conclusions are more likely to influence than indefinite conclusions that enable receivers to connect the dots on their own. Exceptions are receivers, typically top managers, who resent others who attempt to make decisions they are paid to make. The tone of the message often overcomes that roadblock by couching explicit conclusions and recommendations as suggestions or considerations.

In essence, the influence of any message relies heavily on that old standby: Know your audience—its needs, wants, values, and interests—and address them with the content, structure, and tone of your message.

And always remember…the most influential communications are those that are clear, concise, and purposeful/logical… that adhere to the disciplines of good writing. Well-crafted, reasoned communications impress receivers with the sender's intelligence, while poorly crafted communications impress receivers with the sender's ignorance. The result is simply that, assuming other factors to be equal or similar, intelligence, expressed by good communications, wins the sale.

Richard Holbrooke, a distinguished journalist wrote this about George F. Kennan, a very influential employee in the Federal Government: "…Kennan's career suggested that good writing and the study of history—both in short supply in the government—could really matter. No one in government ever wrote better that Kennan, and this was a critical component of his success; the same ideas expressed less cogently by others did not have the same impact."

17. Your unique marketing position and brand: adding power to marketing

Every business has an identity called its brand; here's how to find and exploit it.

Labels change, but often their meanings don't. Take UMP (Unique Marketing Position), Position, and Brand. All are marketers' lingo with identical meanings: the way people, firms, and products are differentiated. Doing so will focus marketing efforts and maximize their positive impact on revenues and profits; not doing so dilutes marketing efforts and negatively impact sales and profits.

All people and organizations market only four traits of their product(s): Quality, Time (or schedule or speed, if you prefer), Information, and Price (Q-TIP) Buyers evaluate and balance Q-TIP in ways that fit their value system. Ergo, the closer a seller's Q-TIP is aligned to the buyer's, the more likely the deal will be sealed.

Here are several examples ranging from personal and universal to professional and specific, all shortened greatly to make the point. One person buys a car first for reliability (the quality most valued), and then price (almost irrelevant for a depreciating asset.). Another buys safety above all and ignores price. Neither cares about time or information.

The Pittsburgh Pirates are an interesting clash of brands. The Pirates literally have in the past marketed poor quality (a losing team), and high quality (a fine ballpark and fireworks) at the same time. They also market low price (tickets are pretty affordable relative to other pro sports), and high price (food and beverages are dear once you are in the park.) They play so many games that time/schedule is not an issue. Given their confusing brand, it's not at all surprising that attendance was near the bottom of both leagues. All that has changed in recent seasons, when the team is marketing exciting and competitive ball.

Perhaps the Pirates have learned from their neighbors, the Pittsburgh Penguins and Steelers. Both field competitive, exciting teams in unexceptional arenas. The price of a ticket is far higher than the price of a ticket to a Pirates game, yet the arenas are packed and fans are lined up to buy more. Time/schedule isn't a factor. Quality wins hands down.

A quick look at other brands: Geico has established itself as the low-price choice for auto insurance, and is now shifting a bit to quality as demonstrated by customer satisfaction ratings. Other insurance companies are following. FedEx markets quality (if it absolutely has to be there) and time (overnight). UPS has followed and is thriving.

One firm in the professional services business prospers by selling a wide range of services based on quality (deliverables meet or exceed specs from day one), and time (this firm claims to have never missed a deadline if the scope of work hasn't been revised by the client). Price is a minor or missing consideration. Perhaps not surprisingly, the latest recession has downsized this firm quite seriously, but it hasn't changed its brand as top managers await the coming upturn.

Another client plays in a single but wide market niche. It markets quality of a different sort (it and its clients have never been sued for irresponsible design), price and time (its engineers know the technology so well that they can design plants efficiently and quickly.) Ideal, wouldn't you say, to offer the entire Q-TIP. This firm has grown by twenty percent during the recession.

A small electrical design firm was founded 15 years ago to sell a combination of price and quality that is rare in any business. The founder is so dedicated to quality, mainly safety, that he will invest more man-hours into a project than he bid, inevitably raising costs and reducing margins. And he refuses to submit drawings to clients that do not meet specs. "Better late than wrong", is one of his mantras; "Better to book less profit than lose a client", is another. This firm has shrunk a bit during the recession, but is recovering nicely by working with clients that respect its business model and ethics.

Finding your own brand: the five-step process for established firms

1. Analyze your winning and losing proposals during the past few years and ask 'why' in every case. Most of us analyze losing proposals to uncover what went wrong; it's just as important to analyze winning proposals to uncover what went right. Eliminate the wrong, reinforce the right.
2. Call selected clients and ask for their take to be sure it agrees with yours. If it does, congratulations; you know your capabilities, customers, and competition. If it doesn't, rethink.
3. Tabulate the results of your analyses under the four traits of Q-TIP. Then define each if those broad traits

with details, some of which are sprinkled in the short case studies above.

4. Decide what your brand really is based on your findings of how clients balance Q-TIP, not how you think they balance it.
5. Shape your proposals, reports, and other marketing materials to comply with and support your brand, which is the balance of Q-TIP that fits your firm and its clients.

Who creates your brand?

Do astute businesspersons create a brand based on their expertise and that of their organizations and push it into the market, or do they examine the market and pull their findings back into their organizations?

Yes.   Push and pull are two sides of the same coin, and both are always in play in varying weights as the business and market evolve.

To review: Every business sells only four traits of its offerings: Quality, Time, Information, and Price, or Q-TIP. Each seller strives to define and balance its Q-TIP in ways that fit its skills and philosophies (its business model), and each buyer must do the same (its business model). When the seller's and buyer's business models are identical or close, the classic win-win is created and the sale is made. If the two Q-TIPS are out of sync, it's back to the drawing board for both parties.

Assume that you are Joe Startup or Mary Recent Entry, and have an idea—every business is started by a person(s) with an idea- for a product/service/skill that you're sure buyers will clamor to buy. But, unlike the erroneous and misleading cliché about customers beating their way to your door to buy a better mousetrap, they won't beat their way to your door unless they know about the wonders of your idea and how it fits within their Q-TIP.

You need a Brand, a Unique Marketing Proposition, a Position, an identity that differentiates and separates you from the crowd, and you need to shout it.

As a startup or early entry you will likely develop your brand using, either consciously or intuitively, a three-step process:

1. You search your mind for recent experiences—a few conversations with potential customers leading the way—and figure you know what's in demand at the moment.
2. You create a sales letter announcing the availability of your product/service/skill and push it into the

market via email or US mail, a few phone calls, lunches, industry meetings and the like.

3. You monitor responses and adjust your Q-TIP appropriately, or you go out of business.

One example: Three engineers with diverse and synergistic disciplines decided about a year ago to band together and form a business   that they named after the discipline that they thought would bring in the most revenue. They conferred to list all the services they could offer, and came up with 117. Not surprisingly, they created a brand of confusion and obfuscation, and a year later they are still struggling and chasing after contracts almost randomly. Their hit rate is a woeful 10 percent and they wonder why. They still don't understand that they don't know what they are offering, and that their potential clients are equally in the dark.

Another example: A young, local consulting firm was modestly successful marketing a single service to a single group of customers, the perfect niche business. The owner decided that revenues and profits were unacceptably stagnant, and he realized that to grow he had to add product lines, which changed his strategic plan and brand, setting off an interesting but typical domino effect. He had to change the name of the firm to reflect its broader product line, which changed all stationary, signage, and marketing materials such as brochures and web sites. And he had to hire the engineers to complete the contracts he expected to win. The firm is recovering nicely from the expense of re-branding and is growing as planned.

18. Relationship marketing: a case study as told by a founder

Nurturing long-term relationships leads to long-term success... combining performance and service

Allegheny Financial began in 1976 with a simple goal that we sustain today: Provide a service that meets the needs and fulfills the aspirations of clients. If that sounds familiar and a bit simplistic, we agree. We understand that our goal is identical to the goal of every business, so we drilled down to be more specific and came up with this: We provide a service that is based on listening carefully and responding appropriately to clients' needs and aspirations and to help them live comfortably, unobstructed with the many and varied hassles of their finances.

Building relationships that last and that proliferate via referrals—we call that the domino effect—has been key to meeting that goal. Along the way, we developed the following imperatives:

Imperative 1. Avoid the one-timers, nurture the long-termers

Money Magazine asked us and a few others to create a financial plan for a 'typical couple' that the editors profiled. We jumped at the national exposure, sure that we would be bombarded with a plethora of opportunities for new clients. Instead, we were bombarded with phone calls from confused folks asking if they should renew a CD or buy IBM or some other minutia that we cannot possibly answer without knowing the goals and aspirations of the callers. When we told them that, they invariably went away: too much effort, not the quick fix they wanted and we are loath to give.

Then pay dirt. A reader of *Money* called from Johnstown PA; he wanted an adviser who would examine his total financial picture and his long-term goals. We started by guiding and supporting him through a complex and harrowing bankruptcy via many personal visits, all at our normal fees. We somehow recognized the potential for a win-win relationship, and we think he did too.

The results: The domino effect in action. After 20 years he is still a client, has referred us to many others in the Johnstown area and in North Carolina, Massachusetts, and Illinois—some 25 in all, at last count—and they have referred us to still others. On a broader scale: almost all our new clients—we estimate 98 percent-- are referrals despite consistent advertising on radio and in print, mainly in arts programs. When we lose a client, which is rare, it's almost always because of death or transfer, not for lackluster performance or service.

Imperative 2.Listen carefully, respond in ways that touch

Back in the mid-nineties a successful entrepreneur came to us with several file boxes full of financial statements and a tale of woe: seems he was collecting at least 45 pieces of random paper a month from this mutual fund, that individual stock, those bond funds, and a bunch of IRS notices that he couldn't decipher even if he had the time, which he didn't. He was spending—wasting, he admits-- hours shuffling papers aimlessly and fruitlessly; he still could not compute his net worth or his income from dividends and interest.

He was harried to the point of distraction, and he wanted desperately to focus on his consulting business, not his money. He put it this way: "I'll make it, you make it work." No question he wanted an adviser.

We went through our usual introductory interview, which literally forced him to list his assets and liabilities. He has never let us forget that our first bit of advice was to buy a new car: "Your car is dangerous, and it won't protect your most valuable asset, the one that's not on your balance sheet: you."

The results, almost 20 years later: By his own admission, he spends maybe 20 minutes at most per month reviewing his portfolio, freeing considerable time for his business and pleasure. He has referred two of his children—which we think of as the ultimate sustainability of our business-- and dozens of his clients to us, and, in another example of the domino effect, his clients and his significant other have followed suit. He and I were at a large party last summer—yes, we are social as well as business friends--and he asked me how many attendees he had referred to me. "A bunch," I replied, "too many to count."

Imperative 3. The soft sell builds, the hard sell diminishes

We have never subscribed to what we call the entertainment or hard side of marketing, the dinners, clubs, golf outings and the like that we feel are so blatantly commercial to the point of arm twisting. We prefer to take our clients to modest lunches at which we tend to discuss topics other than the client's portfolio. We'd rather delve lightly into topics that allow us to know the client better: family, planned major purchases or changes in lifestyle such as retirement or travel, hobbies, and feelings about national or international finances (which help us understand the client's tolerance for risk, for example).

Our client, in turn, learns more about us and our investment philosophies and plans—a classic win-win.

Imperative 4. We're not for everyone, and suspect that you aren't either

"Patience" is my favorite word of advice, and it applies to investing as well as relationship-building. "Aggressive" is my least favorite word of advice, and I use it only to understand a client's tolerance for risk.

Obviously, not every investor wants to be patient. We lost a client recently because he thought we are too conservative, too willing to wait for an upturn in the financial markets. He wasn't for us, and we wish him well.

Our feeling is that no business meets the needs of every client, even those that operate within a narrow niche market. Trying to do so surely dilutes the well-defined focus and mission of the firm.

Imperative 5.   Apply all of the above imperatives to your employees

Our vision is to make a difference in the lives of our clients. Our philosophy with regards to our employees -- truly our firm's most important assets -- has always been quite simple: surround yourself with bright, energetic, innovative people who understand our vision and the importance of delivering excellent client service. Work as a team.

The 98 percent referral rate mentioned earlier is not achieved unless all of the players on the team are working together, and hopefully, enjoying what they do.

Of course, you inevitably begin the employee relationship with an assessment of a fundamental skill set, which is always the easy part, and then all of the above imperatives come into play: nurturing, listening, taking a personal interest, and creating a team that celebrates successes (both emotionally, and of course, we cannot forget monetarily) and analyze the failures to determine what could have been done differently. The long-term relationship building with your team will almost certainly enhance your client relationship-building.

The bottom line

Allegheny has grown from three employees, the original founders, to 85 full-time employees and 50 independent advisers, and from a few dollars under management to more than three billion dollars.

Our ability to build and maintain long-term relationships with clients who fit and agree with our mission has been pivotal, as we feel it can be for most consultants of any type or size.

Epilogue: Our mission is implemented by superior performance and service. Our firm cannot survive on one without the other; we must excel at both to sustain and grow. I think of performance as our hard side, the abilities to uncover, analyze, and recommend investments--the skills we learn in business school-- for clients that meet their strategic needs. Of course that requires critical and creative thinking as we read between the lines of financial statements.

 Service is our human side, andwe subscribe to all the skillsposited in this book to some degree. If pressed, I might say that ethics is most important. We absolutely would be out of business if there was even a hint of unethical behavior in our marketplace. Our clients remember all too well the recent financial meltdowns.

Closely related to ethics is trust, so closely related that we think of them as a single mindset. We agree with Warren Bennis when he wrote, in *On Becoming a Leader,* "...the trust factor will reign as the most pivotal factor in a leader's success."

Treating all stakeholders with dignity is right up at the top of our priorities as well , so much so that we are a chapter in Pete Geissler's book, *The Power of Dignity*.

FURTHER READING

PART V: THINKING

Serious Creativity, by Edward De Bono

Learn Faster and Remember More, by David Gamon and Allen Bragdon

The Power of Writing Well, Pete Geissler

Emotional Intelligence, by Daniel Golman

Thinking For Yourself, by Marlys Mayfield

Thinkertoys, by Michael Muchalko

On Writing, by Stephen King

Thinking Through Writing, by Susan Horton

Writing toLearn, by William Zinsser

Creative Breakthroughs, by Jill Morris

The Courage to Create, by Rollo May

Think Before you Write, by William G. Leary and James Steel Smith

Smart Work, The Syntax Guide for Mutual Understanding in the Workplace, by Lisa Marshall and Lucy Freedman.

PART VI: BEHAVIORS

The 7 Habits Of Highly Effective People, by Stephen R. Covey;

Ethical Reasoning, Dr. Richard Paul and Dr. Linda Elder, The Foundation for Critical Thinking

The Power of Dignity, Pete Geissler

The Power of Ethics, by Pete Geissler and Bill O'Rourke

PEAK, by Chip Conley

Cause for Success, by Christine Arena

PART VII: RELATIONSHIPS

Positioning—The battle for your mind, by Al Reis and Jack Trout.

Leapfrogging the Competition, by Oren Harari.

Competitive Advantage: Creating and Sustaining Superior Performance, by Michael Porter

The Service Organization: Climate is Crucial, Organizational Dynamics, vol. 9, #2.

Relationship Marketing, By Leonard Berry, American Marketing Association.

RELEVANT QUOTES, SOME INSIGHTFUL, SOME HUMOROUS, ALL WORTHY

"Although popularity and affluence, for example, are nice outcomes, people prefer to define *success* as the ability to 'make a difference', 'create lasting impact', and' being engaged in a life of personal fulfillment'". From *Success Built to Last*.

"Management by objective is fine if you know the objectives. Ninety percent of the time you don't." Peter Drucker.

"The computer is a moron." Peter Drucker

"Words are one of our chief means of adjusting to all the situations of life. The better control we have over words, the more successful our adjustment is likely to be." Bergen Evans.

"The root of all bad writing is to compose what you have not worked out for yourself." Alfred Kazan

"Of course, you can't win them all (relationships). You won't be able to—or even want to—keep everyone on your team." From *Success Built to Last*.

"Differentiating a business, e.g. by maintaining long-term relationships for more personal service, can lead to exceptional growth." Anonymous